That Forever Kind of Love

Help your partner to fall in love with you all over again

By Jean Young

EXPERIENCE
EVERYTHING
PUBLISHING

Disclaimer

This document is geared towards providing exact and reliable information in regards to the topic and issue covered. The publication is sold with the idea that the publisher is not required to render accounting, officially permitted, or otherwise, qualified services. If advice is necessary, legal or professional, a practiced individual in the profession should be ordered.

- From a Declaration of Principles which was accepted and approved equally by a Committee of the American Bar Association and a Committee of Publishers and Associations:

The information provided herein is stated to be truthful and consistent, in that any liability, in terms of inattention or otherwise, by any usage or abuse of any policies, processes, or directions contained within is the solitary and utter responsibility of the recipient reader. Under no circumstances will any legal responsibility or blame be held against the publisher for any reparation, damages, or monetary loss due to the information herein, either directly or indirectly.

The information herein is offered for informational purposes solely, and is universal as so. The presentation of the information is without contract or any type of guarantee assurance.

The trademarks that are used are without any consent, and the publication of the trademark is without permission or backing by the trademark owner. All trademarks and brands within this book are for clarifying purposes only and are the owned by the owners themselves, not affiliated with this document.

Introduction

How Relationships Have Changed Over Time

Section 1: Be More Affectionate

Section 2: Go On A Vacation

Section 3: Make Saying Thank You A Habit

Section 4: Compliment Your Partner

Section 5: Limit Use Of Technology

Section 6: Bring The Excitement Back

Section 7: Pursue Personal Interests

Section 8: Pursue An Activity That You'll Both Enjoy

Section 9: Consider Going On Double Dates

Conclusion

Introduction

In your lifetime, you will witness different kinds of relationships. It could be from your own experience, the experience of people around you and those that you see on television or even the internet. Some are blissful and romantic. While others are not so fortunate and are chaotic. Regardless of the experiences that you have had or seen from the people you mingle with, we all want the same thing. We all want to be in a relationship with a partner who can make us happy and a relationship that lasts for a lifetime.

Finding a partner that can last not just the sunny days but the storms with you as well is not an easy thing. Sometimes we have to go through painful and failed relationships before we can finally say that we have found the right one that we want to spend forever with. There are many ways to tell if your partner is really in love with you. And what are these signs? Well, they are listed below.

Signs that will show that your partner is in love with you

1   A partner who loves you will treat you with respect. They won't be criticizing you relentlessly on how you look or act. Rather, they will compliment you instead on the good things: how you look, how you behave, your achievements and so on. If there is any mistake that they need to point out to you which needs to be worked on, they will do it in a manner that will still show that they respects you and not in a way that will make you feel small.

2   No matter how busy their day is, they will always find a minute or two to let you know that they are thinking of you. Even when they is out with their friends, they'll find the time to call you or even send you a text message.

3   When it comes to subjects that both of you have different stands on, your partner will be able to find a way to make a compromise even when they find it difficult to do so. They won't force you to always obey what they say or follow their lead all the time. Rather, they will find a half-way point that both of you can agree on.

4   Being affectionate in private is not a difficult thing to do. However, a partner who can publicly show their affection for you in public is another telltale sign that they loves you. They are not afraid to show to the world that they love you.

5   They will want you to get along with their family and love them like your own. After all, their family will be your family too.

6   Couples fight. Even the happiest couples come across rocky roads too. A person who loves you will not be afraid to say what is on their mind, even if it means that you might get mad at them. Neither will they be afraid to set aside their pride and apologize.

7   Listen to how they talk about your relationship together. They see you and them as a unit. Instead of referring to you the two of you as 'you' and 'me', they would use the words 'we', 'us', 'team' and any other similar terms.

8   Talking about the future is inevitable. When they see you as a part of their future and make plans with you included in it, then you surely have a keeper right there.

9   A person who is in love with you will let you know that they are. And after seeing the other telltale signs that we've mentioned above in them, then believe them instead of doubting them.

Relationships fail for lots of reasons. Sometimes it is because of the different stands they have on a subject. It could be because of lack of honesty, trust or respect. Financial issues can cause a relationship to fall apart too. After you have found your partner, what can you do to make sure that you do your part to make the relationship last?

- Love your partner for who they are and not what you can change them to. Do not be in love with just the idea of loving them either. Love your partner as a whole, including their not so good side.
- A relationship that does include trust can have so many issues. When you don't trust your partner, it is easy for doubts to find their way into your mind. Doubting your partner's actions or intentions is simply not going to make any relationship work. If a relationship is going to last, then trust is a fundamental that cannot be ignored.
- You have to be compatible when it comes to intimacy. If you like being affectionate and they don't, this can cause problems. So if you notice issues like this, it is important that you clear this subject as earl in your relationship as possible.
- Your partner should help you bring out the best in you instead of making you do bad and mean things.
- You have to be nice to your partner. If you have issues with them, do not nag or yell at them about it in public. Discuss any issue that you have in private.
- If issues or conflicts arise, you need to be able to deal with it effectively. Do not set it aside and expect things to work out on its own. If there are any issues, take the time to discuss it without yelling at each other.

- Any relationship is going to go through difficult and trying times. Instead of letting go when the going gets tough, hang in there for each and with each other. It might be difficult while you are still going through the tough times but when you overcome the challenge, you will emerge as a stronger couple who just survived a storm.
- Money is a sensitive issue for any couple. If things are going to work out for the two of you, you need to be able to discuss finances with each other.

Making a relationship last is going to need constant effort and understanding. In the next sections, you will find tips that can help you make your partner fall in love with you again and again. Do not just stop at making them fall in love with you once. But instead, keep the fire burning by making them fall for you repeatedly.

How Relationships Have Changed Over Time

When you look at the younger generation today, their concept of relationships and love are a little different from the concept of people from previous generations. The digital age has allowed couples to stay in touch more often. Text messages are frequently exchanged between couples and conversations can be done over the phone or video-calling. We must admit that this is fairly convenient especially for those who are in a long distance relationship. There is no need to wait for weeks and even months just to hear from your loved one.

But despite the convenience it brings, the digital age has also replaced how love is seen by the younger generation. Love is something that is being taken for granted by many. One can find someone to go on a date with as quickly as one would be able to order pizza. A person who wants to court or date the person they like, merely sends a text or private message until they can get the other person to say yes to a date. So much for effort, huh?

There once was a time when arranged marriages were the trend. Couples from generations past did not have a say who they got to marry and love was not even important. To the people who arranged the marriage, what was more important was the business or maintaining political alliances. Many would stay in a marriage for convenience or because of what they could gain from it.

But this all changed in the Victorian era where love started becoming a need for any marriage to happen. But a man would have to formally court a lady before he could go out with her. Courtships were strictly supervised by the parents or guardian. One could not just drop by and say 'Let's go on a date'. They had to be properly introduced to each other and even if they are already together they cannot immediately announce this to the public.

There are so many tokens and customs of courtships around the world. But as we are quickly advancing in this digital age, the people sticking to such customs are not easy to find. Courtship has become quite generic too: chocolates, flowers, going to the movies and dining at fancy restaurants until you can finally get the person to commit to the relationship. And sometimes, couple do not really commit to the relationship and officially declare themselves as a couple. They claim to be just dating.

There is nothing wrong with the way love and courtship is perceived today. But for the hopeless romantics out there, finding a love story that can rival 'The Notebook' is not an easy to do anymore. Nevertheless, we all have different stories and we definitely have a say on how our love stories turn out to be.

When you are in a relationship that has lasted for several years already, it is easy to lose the spark that you and your partner once had. Suddenly, you are wondering where the intimacy has gone off to. Your partner who used to smother you with their attention and affection is suddenly being so cold to you. And sometimes, it even gets to the point that it feels like you are sleeping with a roommate instead of your romantic partner.

What happened? Is there anything that you can do to rekindle that old flame that once burned so brightly? And the answer to that is...YES! There are things that you can do to help them fall in love with you again and to make the relationship a more intimate and happier one. Want to know how? Then continue reading the next sections to find out.

Section 1: Be More Affectionate

It's been years since you and your partner have been together. You've been sleeping in the same bed for a while now that everything seems to be just routine. The once hot and steamy nights are gone and the lingering looks during dinner are missing too. What can you do?

It's time to bring back the intimacy in your relationship by being more affectionate. Your busy career or the kids and dogs should not only be recipients of your attention. No matter how busy you are, take a little time for a break and pay attention to your partner. Do not always be in a rush to get to work and just settle for that quick peck on the lips or cheek. Physical contact is a very important part of any relationship. Research shows that your body's oxytocin level goes up significantly if you hug or kiss your partner for more than twenty seconds.

Here are some quick facts about oxytocin:

- It is also known as a cuddle or bond hormone.
- Women release great amount of oxytocin during childbirth and while breastfeeding.
- It has a great effect on how you deal with the society but it also depends greatly on the circumstance.
- There are studies that suggest that oxytocin can actually make a man be monogamous, or close to one at least.

So do not just settle for that quick peck. Give your partner that long and calming hug to help release oxytocin to get the bond starting between you again.

Are there other ways to be more affectionate and intimate with each other? Yes, there is. When it comes to intimacy, do not just depend on sex to get that intimacy. When you sleep, opt to sleep closer to each other. When you have a toddler or a dog sleeping in the bed with you, you might want to take a few minutes alone so that you can cuddle with each other. Skin-to-skin sleeping can also increase intimacy and affection.

Section 2: Go On A Vacation For Two

You and your partner might no longer have time alone for each other especially when there are kids involved or if both of you are busy with your careers. If your other responsibilities have prevented you and your partner to spend quality time together, then it is time for you two to take a break from all your responsibilities and give yourselves time to focus on each other alone.

You do not really need to go on an out-of-town trip especially if it is out of your budget. Spend the long weekend at home and if you have kids, drop them off at your parents' place for the weekend so you and your partner can have the house to yourselves without having to worry about your kids.

How can you and your partner benefit from going on a vacation?

- A vacation gives you and your partner to reconnect at a more intimate level. Because it is just you and your partner, you do not have to think about finishing this and that chore. For any romantic relationship to thrive, quality time is needed. So give you and your partner the chance to take a break from your normally hectic days and just sit back and enjoy each other's company. Slow down the pace of your lives for the time of your vacation so that you two have the opportunity to talk about things you normally don't get the chance to talk about. Enjoy taking a stroll at the beach while holding hands. Or if you have chosen to stay at home, cuddle as you watch a movie together.

- You have the opportunity to make more romantic memories that you can cherish forever.

- When you and your partner do not have to think about the things that needs to be done, you have the chance to relax.
- It is definitely the best way to rekindle the flame you once had. You can do so many things together like eating breakfast in bed together, a candlelit bath and so on. Since there is no need to worry about the other responsibilities, you have all the energy to do different things with your partner.
- And last but not the least, you have all the time in the world to have some mind-blowing sex. I mean why not do it since you are on a romantic getaway anyway?

Before you plan that trip though, make sure that you talk to your partner about it so both of you can set expectations and to also help ensure that both of you can get away from work. You do not want to plan a surprise which will only end up being canceled at the last minute, right?

Section 3: Make Saying Thank You A Habit

Another thing that we often overlook is showing our appreciation for our partners every time they do something nice. Because you and your partner have been in a relationship for so long, everything has become a routine. When a light bulb is busted and they have to fix it or when they pick you up from routine, it becomes more of an obligation rather than something to thank them for.

When you say thank you more often to your partner, you are not just showing that you are polite and have good manners. There is more that your relationship and your partner can benefit from with this habit.

1. Saying thank you often enough will make your partner feel appreciated.
2. It can dictate how a relationship will go. A partner who does not feel that their efforts are appreciated is going to start doubting being in the relationship.
3. In tough times like a relationship about to end up in a divorce and a break up, saying thank you and appreciating your partner might prevent that from happening.
4. It can also buffer any negative effects that conflicts in a relationship might have.

So if your partner has done something nice, always make an effort to say thank you and show them that you appreciate the nice thing that they have done. There are many ways to say thank you. A little note that shows your gratitude is one way to do it. And if you feel like making a bit more effort to show your gratitude, reward your partner with something that they like. It can be anything from cooking their favorite dish to tickets to watch their favorite football team playing. Or you can even give them a heartwarming smile and a touch on their arm to show your thanks. Whatever works for you and your partner then do it.

Another advantage of saying thank you is that your partner is going to want to keep doing nice things because they know you appreciate these little things that they do. In the end, your relationship will have more chances of being a happier one because chances are, your partner will show you the same gratitude that you are showing them. In return, you will also experience the same benefits that your partner is getting when you show your gratitude to them.

Section 4: Compliment Your Partner

It is easy to start focusing on the negative aspects of a relationship when you and your partner have been together for quite some time. And this is a good way to make a relationship fail. When you start concentrating on the negative things like how busy they seem to be these days and cannot take you out for dates anymore or how they never compliment you, then problems start to arise. You might start to nag and feel hurt, and both you and your partner will stop getting satisfaction from the relationship.

For these very reasons, it is very important that you do not fall into the habit of not giving your partner compliments. So how should you go about with complimenting your partner?

1. Mix the compliments. Sure, we like hearing compliments. But if we hear the same compliment every day then it might not seem like a genuine compliment anymore. Compliment your partner on how they look but don't just stop there. Every now and then compliment them for the other things that he has like their sense of humor, their dedication to their career or maybe their taste in something like clothes or food.

2. Be honest but do not be too brutally honest. There are some things that are better left unsaid.

3. If an opportunity to compliment your partner arises, do not hesitate to take advantage of the opportunity. This is especially helpful if your partner is in a bad mood but proceed with caution.

4. Do not emotionally cheat on your partner when it comes to compliments. This is especially applicable when you have not given your partner compliments lately. Do not go complementing other members of the opposite sex or same sex if you are gay, etc.

5. When your partner asks, "I do not really look like I am 50, right?" or "Did I handle the situation well?", do not start doing an analysis on the situation. Give your

partner a sincere compliment instead. Chances are your partner is just looking for a reassurance or you have not been giving out enough compliments lately.

6. You should also learn to receive compliments given by your partner.

When giving compliments to your partner, make sure that you do it often enough. If you want to be able to give your partner the best compliments, it is important that you are very much aware of your partner's talents, their accomplishments, what you like most about their physical appearance and so on. This is really important if you want to give your partner compliments that are authentic. When you go on looking for the good things in your spouse, you are less likely to concentrate on the negative part of your marriage or the negative side of your spouse. Do not worry because if you look for the good things then you will surely find it. When you give out your compliment also matters so make sure that you compliment when appropriate. And if you will be complimenting your partner, try to be more specific. Instead of just saying *'Good job with the garden'*, you might want to try *'You've done a great job trimming the lawn and putting the fertilizer in the garden. The garden looks awesome. Thanks honey'*.

Section 5: Limit Use Of Technology

Technology has been very helpful in our lives. Long distance relationships do not need to suffer from communication problems because technology has made it easier for us to stay in touch with people we love that is far away from us. Entertainment and search for information is at the tip of our fingers too.

Despite the many benefits of technology use, it also has its disadvantages. The use of technology can take you away from your partner. When you are using your gadget while you are with your partner, your attention is divided between your partner and your gadget. You might notice yourself asking your partner to repeat what they just said because you did not quite catch it since you were busy commenting on an Instagram post of your friend. This is quite frustrating since your partner is going to feel like you are not paying attention. Sometimes technology is being used as an excuse to get away from a needed discussion between you and your partner.

Not giving your full attention to your partner is definitely not a good thing for many reasons. This is the very reason why limitations on the use of technology should be put in place. It is important that you and your partner sit down and talk about this. When should you and your partner set aside your phones and tablets and when is it okay to use them? It is important that you and your partner have a discussion about this so that the two of you can also spend some quality time together without the distraction of phones constantly beeping. The boundaries that are put in place should depend on what works for both of you.

Section 6: Bring The Excitement Back

Just because a relationship is not new anymore, it does not mean that the excitement and surprises have to go away too. If you want your partner to fall in love with you again or recall what it was like falling in love with you in the beginning, then it is time to start incorporating exciting surprises and activities again in your relationship.

Sure, a routine is good because it provides stability. But routines can get boring and it makes the relationship predictable. And you slowly start getting bored yourself with the relationship and your partner too. And the same thing is applicable for your partner. Bring the excitement back in your relationship and make yourselves fall in love with each other all over again.

So how do you bring back that spark and excitement back in your relationship?

1. Romantic dinners complete with candle lights are fun and romantic. There's no doubt about that. But if this is something that you've been doing for the past months or years that you have been doing, it probably is not as exciting anymore unless you happen to surpass the romantic level of the last dinner date that you had every single time. Ditch the romantic dinner dates and try something else that will literally bring the thrill back in your romance. Try doing activities that can give you and your partner an adrenaline rush like rock/wall climbing, dancing or water sports.

2. Sexual interests can decrease the longer you have been together. Which will explain why sex in the beginning of the relationship is always mind-blowing. So what can you do to make this better? One solution is to have an open relationship. But an open relationship is not something that works for everyone. But even if you stay monogamous, there are still various things that you can do to bring back the spark in your sex life. You can watch porn together or build the sexual tension elsewhere and then finish it off with your partner. The latter does not mean making out with others though then going back to your partner to release the tension.

3. If you've been with your partner for a long time, chances are you know them as well as you know yourself. With this feeling of familiarity, you start feeling like

there is nothing new to discover about each other. But you are wrong. Set you and your partner up for a challenge and do the challenge together. The two of you can decide to work out together to stay in a better shape or be wiser financially. What's important is that you have each other's back especially when it starts becoming difficult.

4. Every now and then take a break from each other. It does not mean that your relationship has to be put on hold or that you should force each other to spend time away from each other. What we mean by this instead is disrupting an activity that you enjoy doing together and finish it a bit later. When you interrupt a routine that you two normally have, you and your partner are also resetting the expectations that both of you have of each other. This is probably all that you need in order to put that excitement back in the relationship.

5. Catching your partner off-guard with a surprise is also a good way to bring the excitement back in your relationship. There are many ways that you can surprise your partner. All you need to do is to find out what they like and surprise them with that.

Section 7: Pursue Your Interests

Your personal interests do not have to be put on hold just because you are in a relationship already. Despite being in a relationship already, it is important that you still continue cultivating things that you find interesting and your partner does not have to be interested in the same thing that you are interested in. Allow your partner too to pursue their interest. When both of you are engaged in your personal interests, you are likely to feel more satisfied with your lives and tend to be happier in general. When your partner is happy and satisfied, they will be able to bring more positive vibes to your relationship and they can pay more attention to you and your relationship too. On the other hand, a person who does not feel contented with their personal life could also bring that negativity to the relationship.

Your partner may have interests that you really can not force yourself to like, no matter how hard you try. And you don't even have to try liking what they like for the sake of the relationship. Allow your partner to do what they like or is passionate about. Instead, be there to support them. The things they are passionate about are the things where they can be in their best. If they likes to go fishing, then just be with them without feeling the need to fish too. You could maybe keep them entertained while you the two of you wait for a bite or help navigate a boat. Being by their side and supporting them in their interests is surely a great way to make them fall for you all over again.

Section 8: Pursue An Activity That You'll Both Enjoy

After you have both decided on pursuing your respective interests, you might also want to start pursuing something that both of you are interested in. Do not just think about things that you are interested in and just assume that your partner not mind hopping on board. Instead, sit down and talk about. Think about the things that both of you are really interested in and pursue that. There are many things that you can do together and the most common option taken is having kids or adopting them and raising them together. Although having children should not be the solution to a failing relationship. However, if you've been-there-done-that or you cannot go down the road of having kids just yet, there are many other options to look into. You can raise a pet together, get into the same sport that you are both interested in, volunteer to do charity work, open up a business. The options are limitless.

When you and your partner work on something, you are increasing the chances of your relationship to last longer. And doing something together allows your partner to see you from a different perspective and vice versa. Doing something that both of you are interested in is also a good way to make both of you happier.

Although on another note, you might also want to give your partner's hobby a try. Sometimes we say no to things without really trying it out first. It might be one of those things that you thought you would not like but actually loved it the moment you tried it out. And what's even better is that you have your own personal teacher to give you lessons on this new hobby and maybe even more. There's no harm really in trying it out and if you realize that it really isn't something you can do, then you can always talk to your partner and continue the search once again for the new hobby. What's important is that you are both in it together.

Section 9: Consider Going On Double Dates

Yes, quality time with each other is important. But going out with your friends or on double dates is good for your relationship too. Why? Here's why:

1. Your partner will be able to see you from another perspective and so will you. You and your partner get the opportunity to observe each other as you interact with the other couple. It is a good way to remind yourselves of things that you love about the other.

2. It gives you and your partner to look even more attractive because chances are you are both going to make an extra effort to dress up.

3. The stories you both have heard often enough suddenly sounds brand new and hilarious now that there are new people listening to these stories.

4. Double dating is a great way to share the history that both you and your partner share and relive those wonderful moments.

5. Dating by yourselves if fun and all but double dates are a great way to take you out of your comfort zone and try something new like a new restaurant that just opened or trying a new activity.

6. Aside from helping put back the spark in an old relationship, double dates also help new relationships become more solid because your partner is able to see you in a different light.

7. It is a good way to remind each other of the reasons why you fell in love with each other in the first place.

8. Double dates can help you get through rocky times.

9. It's fun.

Conclusion

Relationships have ups and downs. Being with the same person for a long time can give us a sense of familiarity and stability. But sometimes, we start getting so used to having the other person around that everything starts becoming a routine. We do things automatically because it's what we are used to or it is what we think the other expects of us. And couples then start forgetting why they fell in love with each other because they start focusing on other aspects like the flaws of their partner. When this happens, the relationship is placed in a situation where it could fall apart any time.

If you want your relationship to last and be a happy one, the efforts that you exert to make your partner love you should not stop the moment you two become a couple. Every now and then, you need to do things and say things that will remind you and your partner why you are in the relationship in the first place. No couple is ever too old for a little flirting and affection. And your partner can never get too many compliments when it comes from you. You do not have to go on a trip to Mars and back in order to make your partner fall in love with you over and over again. There are many little things that you can do to keep the flame alive in your relationship and to turn your relationship into something that is worth keeping for a lifetime.

So what are you waiting for? It's time to put in some extra effort to get your partner swooning over you all over again and be on your road to forever.

EXPERIENCE
EVERYTHING
PUBLISHING

www.ingramcontent.com/pod-product-compliance
Lightning Source LLC
Chambersburg PA
CBHW071812020426
42331CB00008B/2470